G A O
Accountability * Integrity * Reliability

Highlights

Highlights of GAO-12-441, a report to congressional committees

PROLIFERATION SECURITY INITIATIVE

Agencies Have Adopted Policies and Procedures but Steps Needed to Meet Reporting Requirement and to Measure Results

I0409649

Why GAO Did This Study

In 2003, the Bush Administration announced the Proliferation Security Initiative (PSI) to enhance U.S. efforts to prevent the spread of weapons of mass destruction (WMD). PSI is not a program housed in only one agency, but instead is a set of activities with participation by multiple U.S. agencies and other countries. Congress recommended that the Department of Defense (DOD) and Department of State (State) establish policies, procedures, and indicators to measure results and required that they submit annual reports. It also mandated that GAO report on PSI effectiveness. In 2008, GAO likewise recommended that law enforcement agencies also establish policies, procedures, and performance indicators.

This report assesses (1) the progress relevant agencies have made since 2008 in establishing recommended PSI policies and procedures and issuing required annual reports; and (2) the extent to which PSI activities have enhanced and expanded U.S. counterproliferation efforts.

GAO reviewed and analyzed agency documents and interviewed officials from State, DOD, and other agencies with PSI responsibilities.

What GAO Recommends

GAO recommends that State and DOD provide all required expenditure information in PSI annual reports and develop a framework for measuring PSI's results. DOD partially concurred with both recommendations and State partially concurred with the reporting recommendation. State disagreed with the framework recommendation, but noted its support for analysis consistent with it.

View GAO-12-441. For more information, contact Thomas Melito at (202) 512-9601 or melitot@gao.gov.

What GAO Found

U.S. agencies have adopted interagency guidance documents that establish PSI policies and procedures and have submitted annual reports; however, these reports do not contain expenditure data for all agencies as required by law. The agencies produced documents that contain general PSI policies and procedures. In addition, DOD and the Department of Homeland Security's Customs and Border Protection (CBP) developed policies and procedures specifically to guide their agencies' PSI activities. The annual reports submitted in 2009, 2010, and 2011 met requirements to describe PSI-related activities planned for future years and those that took place in the preceding year. Although the reports included an account of DOD's PSI expenditures, they did not contain all expenditures for other agencies for PSI activities as required by law.

U.S. officials participated in a range of PSI activities since 2008 to meet their objective of expanding and enhancing counterproliferation efforts, but it is unclear to what extent these activities have achieved the objective because agencies lack measures of results. The agencies either led or participated in 22 PSI activities from fiscal year 2009 through fiscal year 2011 including multilateral meetings and exercises. Officials stated that their outreach efforts contributed to increased support for PSI since GAO's 2008 report, such as the increase from 93 to 98 countries endorsing PSI. In addition, they have extended access to PSI activities to more countries that are not part of the group of 21 PSI Operational Experts Group countries, for example by holding regional planning meetings. Despite recommendations of Congress and GAO that agencies develop PSI performance indicators, DOD, State, CBP, and the Federal Bureau of Investigation have not developed indicators that can be used to systematically measure progress toward the stated PSI objective. Further, the agencies have not systematically evaluated PSI activity results. Although some officials indicated plans to develop PSI performance indicators, officials from DOD and State also cited several challenges to developing indicators to measure PSI activities' results including difficulty quantifying how PSI activities improved capacity. However, GAO has previously reported that, despite such challenges, developing measures that help link activities to results is possible. PSI agencies could develop a framework that links performance measures to outcomes. For example, such a framework could link the number of participants trained to changes in national policies that strengthen participant countries' authority to interdict the shipment of WMD, their delivery systems, and related materials.

_____ United States Government Accountability Office

Contents

Tables

Figure

Abbreviations

9/11 Act	Implementing Recommendations of the 9/11 Commission Act of 2007
CBP	Customs and Border Protection
CCP	Critical Capabilities and Practices
DHS	Department of Homeland Security
DOD	Department of Defense
DOE	Department of Energy
DOJ	Department of Justice
FBI	Federal Bureau of Investigation
OEG	Operational Experts Group
PSI	Proliferation Security Initiative
State	Department of State
Treasury	Department of the Treasury
WMD	weapons of mass destruction

G A O

Accountability * Integrity * Reliability

United States Government Accountability Office
Washington, DC 20548

March 27, 2012

Congressional Committees

For almost 10 years, the United States has been actively participating in the Proliferation Security Initiative (PSI) to assist in U.S. efforts to break up black markets, detect and intercept weapons of mass destruction (WMD) materials in transit, and use financial tools to disrupt this dangerous trade. The U.S. government issued the *National Strategy to Combat Weapons of Mass Destruction* in 2002, and the proliferation of WMD, such as nuclear- or missile-related goods or technology, remains one of today's key challenges to international security.[1] In May 2003, President Bush announced PSI, a multinational effort, including the United States, to focus on building WMD interdiction capabilities by endorsing the *Statement of Interdiction Principles*. According to the Department of State (State), PSI's objective is to enhance and expand U.S. efforts to prevent the flow of WMD, their delivery systems, and related materials on the ground, in the air, and at sea, to and from states and nonstate actors of proliferation concern. The current administration has continued to support PSI, and agencies with PSI responsibilities have reaffirmed that objective. Furthermore, the administration has declared PSI an important global tool for countering the spread of WMD-related materials, while President Obama has called for it to be turned into a "durable international institution."[2]

In our September 2006 report on PSI, we found that U.S. agencies did not have the policies and procedures in place to plan and manage their PSI activities or performance indicators to measure their results. We recommended that they correct these deficiencies. Following our report, Congress passed the Implementing Recommendations of the 9/11 Commission Act of 2007 (the 9/11 Act), in which it expresses its sense that relevant agencies and departments take actions to expand and strengthen PSI, including establishing clear PSI policies and procedures

---

[1]For example, a North Korean cargo ship was reportedly suspected of carrying short-range missiles to Burma in late May 2011. See *Arms Control Today* (July 2011-August 2011).

[2]See President Obama's remarks in Prague, Czech Republic, April 5, 2009.

and performance indicators to measure the results of PSI activities.[3] The 9/11 Act also required DOD and State to submit annual PSI reports and mandated GAO to assess and report periodically on PSI's effectiveness, including progress made in implementing the law's provisions. In 2008, we reported that agencies had taken some steps but needed to do more to strengthen and expand PSI, such as taking actions on some of the law's provisions.[4] This report updates and provides information on the agencies' actions and the progress evaluating PSI since our 2008 report. Specifically, this report assesses (1) the progress relevant agencies have made since 2008 in establishing recommended PSI policies and procedures and issuing required annual reports; and (2) the extent to which PSI activities have enhanced and expanded U.S. counterproliferation efforts.

To assess what agencies have done since 2008 to establish recommended PSI policies and procedures and issue required annual reports, we reviewed the findings and recommendations in GAO's 2006 and 2008 reports on PSI and the congressional mandate. We reviewed documentation of policies and procedures developed since 2008. We also requested and reviewed annual reports submitted to Congress by State and the Department of Defense (DOD) and analyzed them for compliance with the requirements in the 9/11 Act. We reported expenditure data as it appeared in the annual reports to Congress and determined the data were sufficiently reliable for the purposes of our report. To assess how PSI activities have enhanced and expanded U.S. efforts to prevent the flow of WMD materials and to determine what actions, if any, agencies have taken to develop indicators of PSI's success, we reviewed and analyzed documents from DOD, State, the Department of Homeland Security (DHS), and the Department of Justice (DOJ). For both objectives, we also interviewed relevant officials from those agencies. (See app. I for a detailed discussion of our scope and methodology.)

We conducted this performance audit from June 2011 to March 2012 in accordance with generally accepted government auditing standards. Those standards require that we plan and perform the audit to obtain

---

[3]Pub. L. 110-53, sec. 1821(d).

[4]See GAO, *U.S. Agencies Have Taken Some Steps, but More Effort Is Needed to Strengthen and Expand the Proliferation Security Initiative,* GAO-09-43 (Washington, D.C.: Nov. 10, 2008).

sufficient, appropriate evidence to provide a reasonable basis for our findings and conclusions based on our audit objectives. We believe that the evidence obtained provides a reasonable basis for our findings and conclusions based on our audit objectives.

Background

PSI is a multinational effort to prevent the trafficking of WMD, their delivery systems, and related materials to and from states and nonstate actors of proliferation concern. PSI has no formal organization or bureaucracy. In the United States, PSI is not a program housed in a single agency, but instead is a set of activities with participation by seven agencies and the intelligence community.[5] PSI encourages partnership among states to work together to develop a broad range of legal, diplomatic, economic, military, law enforcement, and other capabilities to prevent WMD-related air, land, or sea transfers to states and nonstate actors of proliferation concern. International participation is voluntary, and there are no binding treaties on those who choose to participate. Countries supporting PSI are expected to endorse PSI principles, embodied in four broad goals in the *Statement of Interdiction Principles* of September 2003, by a voluntary, nonbinding "political" commitment to those principles. See appendix II for the full text of the *Statement of Interdiction Principles*. They also voluntarily participate in PSI activities according to their own capabilities. According to the principles, PSI participants use existing national and international authorities to put an end to WMD-related trafficking and take steps to strengthen those authorities, as necessary.

The U.S. government's PSI efforts involve participation in three broad activities: multilateral PSI planning meetings called Operational Experts Group (OEG) meetings, PSI exercises, and other efforts to encourage support and capacity for interdictions, such as workshops and

---

[5]U.S. agencies participating in PSI are the Departments of Defense, State, Homeland Security, Justice, Energy, Commerce, and the Treasury.

conferences.[6] According to State, at multilateral PSI planning meetings, military, law enforcement, intelligence, legal, and diplomatic experts from the United States and other OEG countries meet to consider ways to enhance the WMD interdiction capabilities of PSI participants, build support for the initiative, develop operational concepts, organize PSI exercises, and share information about national legal authorities. The policy office in the Office of the Secretary of Defense heads the U.S. delegation to these multilateral meetings.

PSI exercises vary in size and complexity, and some involve military personnel and assets from participating PSI countries. Other exercises examine the use of law enforcement or customs authorities to stop WMD proliferation. There are also "tabletop" exercises or simulations, which explore scenarios and determine solutions for hypothetical land, air, or sea interdictions. Among the most visible PSI exercises are those that combine a tabletop and a live interdiction exercise using military assets from multiple PSI countries, such as practicing the tracking and boarding of a target ship.

Other activities include both outreach to countries that have not endorsed PSI principles and cooperation and collaboration with countries that have endorsed PSI and are seeking assistance to increase their capacity to act in accordance with the *Statement of Interdiction Principles*. These efforts include workshops, training, conferences, and bilateral discussions with foreign government officials. U.S. officials said they engage in bilateral discussions, for example, to conclude PSI shipboarding agreements or to seek ways to overcome obstacles to support for PSI principles. State takes the lead in diplomatic outreach efforts.

---

[6]The 21 OEG countries are Argentina, Australia, Canada, Denmark, France, Germany, Greece, Italy, Japan, the Netherlands, New Zealand, Norway, Poland, Portugal, Republic of Korea, Russia, Singapore, Spain, Turkey, United Kingdom, and the United States. According to State officials, the OEG is the steering committee for the initiative and participants are generally best positioned to routinely contribute to and host PSI activities, share best practices, and provide lessons learned on activities. OEG meetings provide an essential coordination function and are a venue for nations to discuss counterproliferation interdiction in a multinational setting.

Agencies Have Adopted Policies and Procedures, but Annual Reports Lack Some Required Information

U.S. agencies have adopted interagency guidance documents that establish policies and procedures for all agencies participating in PSI activities. In addition, agencies have submitted annual reports, though they lacked required estimated and actual expenditure information from most participating agencies.

Interagency PSI Policies and Procedures Established

The 9/11 Act expresses Congress' sense that DOD and State should establish, among other things, clear policies and procedures and roles and responsibilities for PSI.[7] As we noted in our 2008 report, while DOD and Customs and Border Protection (CBP) had established some policies and procedures for their PSI activities, State and some law enforcement agencies had not.[8] Since then, an interagency group, including representatives from all agencies participating in PSI, produced two companion guidance documents, *Guidance for U.S. Government Activities in Support of the Proliferation Security Initiative* and *Insuring the Durability of PSI: An Action Plan*, that the interagency group adopted in 2010 and 2011, respectively.[9] According to National Security Staff officials, these documents are a primary source of policies and procedures for all relevant agencies—defining PSI activities, providing guidance on interagency communication, and addressing objectives and responsibilities.[10] For example, they establish that State has primary responsibility for diplomatic outreach activities and that DOD leads the U.S. delegation at OEG meetings.[11] According to officials, such

---

[7]Pub. L. 110-53, sec. 1821.

[8]In our 2008 report, since PSI activities had been increasingly focused on law enforcement issues, we recommended that some law enforcement agencies also establish clear PSI policies and procedures. These agencies concurred with our recommendation.

[9]See appendix I for more information on GAO's access to these interagency policy documents.

[10]While not otherwise directly involved in PSI activities, the National Security Staff participates in interagency meetings and is the official custodian of these documents.

[11]Within DOD, the Office of the Secretary of Defense for Policy is directly responsible for this function.

interagency policies and procedures also allow all U.S. agencies involved in PSI to plan activities without duplicating efforts and to properly and coherently articulate the U.S. government's vision and strategy on PSI.

In addition to interagency guidance, DOD and CBP also have their own PSI-specific policy documents. As we reported in our 2008 review of PSI, DOD had PSI-specific policies and procedures in place, specifically those encouraging combatant command participation in PSI exercises.[12] DOD Joint Staff provided guidance directing combatant commands to leverage the staff, assets, and resources of the existing DOD exercise program in support of PSI exercises. This Joint Staff guidance provided procedures, including roles and responsibilities, for the planning and execution of U.S. military support to PSI. Among other things, the guidance encouraged combatant commands to change existing DOD exercises by adding a PSI component. Our 2008 review also reported that CBP, a component of DHS, produced a PSI-specific directive that provides roles and responsibilities, policies and procedures, and PSI-relevant definitions. Approved in 2006, CBP is currently revising this document to reflect updated roles and responsibilities.

Agencies Submitted Reports, but They Lacked Some Required Information

The 9/11 Act required DOD and State to submit to Congress in February an annual comprehensive joint report, beginning in 2008.[13] The report is to consist of a 3-year plan describing PSI-related activities and identifying estimated expenditures for these activities, and a description of the PSI-related activities and associated expenditures carried out during the fiscal year preceding the year of the report.[14] DOD and State co-author each report, although responsibility for leading the annual effort alternates

---

[12]Through DOD's Joint Staff, we submitted questions to and received responses from the following DOD combatant commands: U.S. Africa Command, U.S. Central Command, U.S. European Command, U.S. Northern Command, U.S. Pacific Command, U.S. Southern Command, and U.S. Strategic Command.

[13]Pub. L. 110-53, sec. 1821(b). The 9/11 Act required that the 2008 report include a description of PSI-related activities carried out during the 3 fiscal years preceding the year of the report, and for the reports submitted in 2009 and each year thereafter, a description of the PSI-related activities carried out during the fiscal year preceding the year of the report. In November 2008, GAO reported that the relevant agencies had not submitted the 2008 report as required.

[14]The 3-year plan in each report is to begin with the fiscal year for the current budget request; for example, the 2011 report includes a 3-year plan covering fiscal years 2012 to 2014.

between the two. The lead agency solicits input from all U.S. agencies participating in PSI and consolidates the information provided to produce the final report for submission to Congress. State and DOD have submitted annual PSI reports in 2009, 2010, and 2011 including descriptions of PSI activities, but these reports do not include all required estimated expenditures for PSI activities over the next 3 fiscal years and the amount expended in the prior year.[15]

DOD is the only agency performing PSI activities that has provided all required planned and prior year expenditure information for these reports. For example, the 2011 report includes information from DOD stating that it plans to conduct a regional PSI exercise called Leading Edge in Central Asia in fiscal year 2012 and in the Middle East in fiscal year 2014 and that each exercise is estimated to cost $600,000 for staff travel to support planning events and exercise execution. Table 1 shows annual planned expenditures from that report for PSI-related exercises in fiscal years 2012 to 2014 for DOD combatant commands and Joint Staff only, including many of the major PSI-related activities expected in that period. The report indicates that these expenditures include travel expenses, conference hosting fees, contracting support, training expenses, and other uniquely PSI-attributable expenses and lists all agencies consulted in the preparation of the report.[16]

---

[15]According to DOD officials, all three reports were submitted to Congress after the February deadline due to interagency coordination issues. For example, the 2011 report was submitted about 6 months late, in September 2011.

[16]The 2011 report states that the following U.S. departments and agencies were consulted in the preparation of the report: DOD, including the Office of the Secretary of Defense, the Joint Staff, and pertinent combatant commands; State; DHS, including CBP, U.S. Coast Guard, and Immigration and Customs Enforcement; the Department of the Treasury; the Department of Energy, including the National Nuclear Security Administration; DOJ, including the Federal Bureau of Investigation; the Department of Commerce; and the intelligence community.

Table 1: Annual Estimated Expenditures for Department of Defense Support to PSI-Related Exercises and Other Events, Fiscal Years 2012-2014

Expenditures rounded to nearest thousands

Fiscal year	Anticipated activities	Total estimated expenditures
2012	• Approximately 1 Operational Experts Group (OEG) meeting • Approximately 3 regional OEG meetings • U.S. Central Command (CENTCOM) - 1 regional exercise • U.S. Pacific Command (PACOM) - 1 regional exercise • U.S. Southern Command (SOUTHCOM) – 1 PSI scenario in 1 exercise • U.S. European Command (EUCOM) - unspecified • U.S. Africa Command (AFRICOM) - 2 PSI scenarios in 2 exercises	$1,063,000
2013	• Approximately 1 OEG meeting • Approximately 3 regional OEG meetings • U.S. Pacific Command (PACOM) - 1 regional exercise • U.S. Southern Command (SOUTHCOM) – 1 PSI scenario in 1 exercise • U.S. European Command (EUCOM) - unspecified • U.S. Africa Command (AFRICOM) - 1 PSI scenario in 1 exercise	$1,123,000
2014	• Approximately 1 OEG meeting • Approximately 3 regional OEG meetings • U.S. Central Command (CENTCOM) - 1 regional exercise • U.S. Pacific Command (PACOM) - 1 regional exercise • U.S. Southern Command (SOUTHCOM) – 1 PSI scenario in 1 exercise • U.S. European Command (EUCOM) - unspecified • U.S. Africa Command (AFRICOM) - 1 PSI scenario in 1 exercise	$973,000

Source: GAO analysis of the 2011 PSI annual report to Congress.

Note: Amounts above represent estimated expenditures for DOD's combatant command and Joint Staff support. They reflect minimum anticipated annual expenditures and do not account for unknown funding requirements resulting from future exercises and other activities hosted by PSI partner nations.

In addition, DOD has fully reported its prior year expenditures and, in many cases, includes expenditure amounts by activity. For example, the 2011 report states that DOD's total PSI expenditures for that year were approximately $519,000. Further, the report includes activity-specific expenditure information, such as the $31,400 DOD spent for training aids and staff travel in support of the Phoenix Express PSI exercise.[17]

---

[17]DOD amounts do not include expenditures for pay and salaries, ship fuel, other operating costs of military assets, or general overhead costs related to the offices and departments whose personnel participate in PSI activities.

The annual reports do not uniformly include expenditure data for any other agencies participating in PSI. For example, the 2010 report states that the United States hosted an OEG meeting in Miami, Florida, for which the United States had a delegation of 34 representatives from DOD, State, DHS, the Federal Bureau of Investigation (FBI), the Department of the Treasury (Treasury), and the Department of Energy (DOE), among others. The report states that DOD contributed about $145,000 but does not include expenditure data from other agencies for the event. Table 2 shows the extent to which PSI annual reports include expenditure information for U.S. agencies participating in PSI activities.

Table 2: Prior Year Expenditure Data Included in Annual Reports to Congress

	2009 report	2010 report[a]	2011 report[a]
DOD	Yes	Yes	Yes
State	Partial	No	No
DHS	No	No[b]	No
DOJ (FBI)	No	Partial	No
DOE	Yes	Yes	No
Treasury	Yes	No	No
Commerce	Yes	No	———[c]

Source: GAO analysis of PSI annual reports to Congress.

[a]The 2010 and 2011 reports state that all unreported expenditure amounts in fiscal years 2009 and 2010 were for PSI-related travel.

[b]DHS provided its PSI expenditures to State for the 2010 report; however, these data were not included in the report.

[c]There is no indication in the report that Commerce participated in PSI activities this year.

Although reports contain some expenditure data from agencies other than DOD, none of the other agencies provide this data for all of the annual reports. For example, for fiscal years 2008 and 2009, DOE reported total PSI expenditures of $69,000 and $55,000 respectively. Also, FBI reported that it spent a total of about $750,000 to organize and sponsor PSI events in Hungary and Australia in fiscal year 2009. However, no expenditure data were provided for activities in which DOE participated for fiscal year 2010 and for FBI's activities in fiscal years 2008 and 2010. From DHS, CBP officials could document submitting PSI-specific expenditures of about $35,000 for the 2010 report; however, the report did not include this information, stating that the only costs DHS incurred were associated with travel to PSI events.[18] According to State officials, State does not identify and track its PSI-related expenditures because it made the decision that such a breakout is unnecessary. However, officials said they could calculate State's total PSI-related expenditures because these are almost entirely for travel to OEG meetings or bilateral negotiations. FBI officials also reported that they do not separately track PSI expenditures.

Of the four agencies we spoke with, only DOD makes a specific budget request for PSI-related activities. U.S. Strategic Command has a fiscal year 2011 budget of $800,000 to provide financial assistance for combatant commanders to plan, participate in, and execute WMD interdiction exercises. This fund is used routinely but not exclusively to support PSI activities such as hosting a PSI exercise, embedding PSI scenarios into broader military exercises, ensuring that appropriate subject matter experts can participate in PSI exercises, or purchasing interdiction-related training aids. According to State officials, they prefer funding PSI expenditures from their general operating accounts because this practice allows them greater flexibility and the ability to fund PSI-related travel when the need arises. FBI and CBP officials also reported that they provide PSI funding when necessary through more general operating accounts.[19]

Agencies that do not track and report their expenditures are not providing Congress sufficient information for Congress to assess U.S. participation in PSI. If agencies are unable to provide requested assistance, but are not tracking or reporting on expenditures, it is difficult for the agencies to determine and demonstrate to Congress whether they are effectively prioritizing their use of limited resources. For example, FBI officials stated they could not provide PSI-related training requested in 2011 by Colombian national police because they did not have sufficient funding.[20]

---

[18]CBP officials also provided documentation of having submitted PSI-specific expenditure data for inclusion in the 2012 report.

[19]FBI draws funding for its PSI-related expenditures from its External Policy and Planning Unit budget. CBP draws funding for its PSI-related expenditures from its Security Initiatives budget.

[20]In this case, FBI officials were able to use the PSI network to put the Colombian officials in contact with officials from Spain's law enforcement community who already scheduled relevant training for Latin American countries.

Moreover, the lack of required expenditure information limits Congress' ability to oversee agencies' commitment to the PSI objective.

Extent to Which Activities Meet PSI Objective Is Unclear because Agencies Lack Measures of Results

DOD, State, CBP, and FBI officials participated in a range of PSI activities since 2008 to meet their objective of expanding and enhancing counterproliferation efforts, but it is unclear to what extent these activities have achieved the objective because agencies lack measures of results. The agencies either led or participated in 22 PSI activities from fiscal year 2009 through fiscal year 2011, including multilateral meetings and exercises. In addition, they have extended access to PSI activities to more countries that are not part of the 21-country OEG. Despite recommendations in the 9/11 Act and by GAO that agencies develop PSI performance indicators, DOD, State, CBP, and FBI have not developed indicators that can be used to systematically measure progress toward the stated PSI objective.[21] Further, the agencies have not systematically evaluated PSI activity results. Although some officials indicated plans to develop PSI performance indicators, officials from DOD and State also cited several challenges to developing indicators to measure PSI activities' results, including difficulty quantifying how PSI activities improved capacity. However, GAO has previously reported that, despite challenges, evaluating results and developing measures are possible. One approach PSI agency officials could consider is developing a framework to link performance measures, such as number of participants trained, to outcomes, such as changes in national policies that strengthen their authority to perform interdictions.

U.S. Agencies Participated in PSI Activities to Support PSI's Objective

PSI's objective is to enhance and expand our capacity to prevent the flow of WMD, their delivery systems, and related materials on the ground, in the air, and at sea, to and from states and nonstate actors of proliferation concern. Agency officials provided us with a range of PSI activities they have participated in since our 2008 report to support the PSI objective. U.S. agencies led or participated in 22 PSI activities from fiscal year 2009 through fiscal year 2011 and State officials reported numerous informal bilateral consultations designed to provide tools that increase countries'

---

[21]In our 2008 report, we specifically recommended that relevant law enforcement agencies work toward developing performance indicators because of the increasing focus of PSI activities on law enforcement issues. DHS and FBI concurred with this recommendation.

capacity to interdict illicit shipments of WMDs and WMD-related materials. As table 3 shows, these activities fall under the three broad categories of the U.S. government's PSI efforts: multilateral OEG meetings, PSI exercises, and other activities such as workshops and training sessions. See appendix III for a summary of each of the PSI activities with U.S. participation from fiscal year 2009 to December 2011. For example, the U.S. Naval Forces Africa hosted an exercise in May 2010 that included a PSI maritime interdiction scenario designed to improve regional cooperation and maritime security in the Mediterranean basin. Also, a U.S. delegation participated in an Australia-hosted exercise in September 2010 that focused on an aircraft counterproliferation scenario and associated customs and law enforcement authorities and challenges. A regional PSI planning meeting was held in conjunction with the exercise.

Table 3: Number and Type of PSI Activities with U.S. Participation, Fiscal Years 2009-2011

Activity type	FY 2009	FY 2010	FY 2011
Multilateral meeting	2	0	1
Exercise	3	3	4
Other activity[a]	1	0	1
Multilateral meeting and other activity	2	0	1
Exercise and other activity	0	0	3
Multilateral meeting and exercise	0	1	0
Total	8	4	10

Source: GAO analysis of DOD and State data.

[a]Other activities include, for example, workshops and training sessions.

Officials from DOD, State, DHS, and FBI stated that their outreach efforts, including State's diplomatic efforts, have contributed to an increased number of countries supporting PSI since our 2008 report. For example, the number of countries that became PSI countries by endorsing the *Statement of Interdiction Principles* has increased from 93 to 98 since 2008 and DOD officials said that they have ongoing efforts with several non-endorsing countries and believe that the number of endorsing countries will continue to rise. The most recent endorsees are Antigua and Barbuda, Colombia, the Republic of Korea (South Korea), St. Vincent and the Grenadines, and Vanuatu. Further, the number of signed bilateral shipboarding agreements between the United States and individual PSI countries increased between November 2008 and February 2012 from 9 to 11.[22] Bilateral shipboarding agreements put procedures into place and identify points of contact to permit the timely inspection by either party of vessels flying their flags suspected of transporting proliferation-related cargo. State officials said these agreements are significant because they have been signed by countries with some of the largest ship registries.[23]

U.S. agencies, in cooperation with the 20 other OEG countries, also have extended access to PSI activities to additional countries since our last report. In 2008, we reported that U.S. agencies had not built relationships with PSI countries that are not OEG countries by involving them in PSI planning and activities. We recommended that U.S. agencies work in conjunction with other leading PSI countries to increase cooperation, coordination, and information exchange with PSI countries that were not invited to multilateral OEG planning meetings.[24] In May 2009, the countries of the OEG committed to consider ways to involve more countries in future PSI planning meetings. According to U.S. officials, they also agreed to increase the number of PSI activities, including regional PSI planning meetings, that include PSI-endorsing countries beyond the OEG countries and, in some cases, non-endorsing countries. In addition, the 2011 U.S. interagency PSI report to Congress stated that activities planned for fiscal years 2012 through 2014 are designed to increase cooperation, coordination, and information exchange with the broad range of PSI-endorsing countries beyond the countries that normally participate in the OEG.

U.S. officials provided examples of expanded efforts to cooperate with non-OEG countries. For example:

---

[22]In addition to the shipboarding agreements signed in 2010 with Antigua and Barbuda and St. Vincent and the Grenadines, the United States also has agreements with The Bahamas, Belize, Croatia, Cyprus, Liberia, Malta, Marshall Islands, Mongolia, and Panama.

[23]A country's ship registry includes vessels that sail bearing the flag of that country. Many of the countries with the largest ship registries have open registries, meaning they engage in the business practice allowing ships to be registered with their country and fly their flag even when the ship owners are from another country. The ability to interdict a shipment depends, in part, on the legal authorities of the country whose flag a ship is flying and vulnerabilities in legal codes may be exploited by merchants shipping WMD or WMD-related materials.

[24]GAO-09-43.

- Eight of the 17 participating delegations at a PSI activity hosted in September 2010 by Australia represented countries not normally invited to multilateral PSI planning meetings. The activity included an aircraft counterproliferation scenario exercise and a regional PSI planning meeting.

- According to U.S. officials, the Republic of Korea endorsed PSI in May 2009 as a result of its participation in PSI activities and became one of the 21 leading PSI countries in November 2010. It organized a PSI exercise and hosted a regional PSI workshop in 2010.

U.S. officials said they are also currently developing the Critical Capabilities and Practices effort, a clearinghouse for PSI-related information and tools, designed to make PSI lessons learned and best practices available both to PSI activity participants and to endorsing countries that were unable to participate in the activities.[25] The OEG countries discussed and confirmed support for the development of the Critical Capabilities and Practices effort. Officials said they have not set a target date for the effort to begin making PSI-related information and tools available.

U.S. Agencies Have Not Established a Framework to Measure PSI's Results

While U.S. agencies have undertaken a range of PSI efforts since 2008, they have not established a framework to measure PSI activities' results and, therefore, it is unclear to what extent these activities have enhanced and expanded capacity to prevent the flow of WMD, their delivery systems, and related materials on the ground, in the air, and at sea, to and from states and nonstate actors of proliferation concern. The 9/11 Act recommended that DOD and State establish indicators to measure results of their PSI activities. It is the responsibility of the implementing agencies to measure the results of PSI activities. Linking the activities to the initiative's overall objective could help the agencies better organize and prioritize future activities. In 2008, we reported that agencies had not established PSI performance indicators. We also recommended that law enforcement agencies, such as DHS and FBI, which we found to have become increasingly involved in PSI activities, establish PSI performance indicators and they concurred.

---

[25]Officials report that the Critical Capabilities and Practices effort will include documentation of past activities and notice of future activities.

The four agencies we reviewed have not established formal performance indicators that can be used to systematically measure progress toward the stated PSI objective. DOD officials said they have general counterproliferation goals but have not developed PSI indicators.[26] FBI officials said that they have performance measures applying to activities of their Weapons of Mass Destruction Directorate, and that their PSI-specific goal is the commitment to participate in PSI activities as appropriate, including at least one PSI exercise per year. Although FBI officials consider this to be a performance indicator, participation alone does not provide information to measure the results of PSI activities. State has identified as its PSI indicator "An Effective Global Network Countering WMD Proliferation-Related Trafficking."[27] However, the measures used to track the indicator's progress change from year to year, making it difficult for State to assess systematically the results of its PSI activities. For example, although State did not meet its fiscal year 2009 target to have 100 PSI-endorsing countries, it did not set targets for the number of PSI endorsees for fiscal years 2010 or 2011. We reported in 2008 that CBP developed a PSI Implementation Plan with expected goals and targets, but that it had not been updated since June 2006.[28] As of February 2012, CBP officials stated that many of the goals are outdated and that the plan has not been updated because they wanted to wait and align their plan with the interagency PSI policy documents that were completed in 2010 and 2011. The officials acknowledged that performance measurement is important and said they are working to include indicators in their updated plan.

In addition, although some agencies have made efforts to assess individual PSI activities, the four agencies we reviewed have not performed a systematic evaluation of the results of PSI activities. Some officials draft summary reports following individual activities to identify issues to address in planning for future activities. For example, FBI

---

[26]Officials from DOD's U.S. Southern Command (USSOUTHCOM) reported that they anticipate working with the U.S. Strategic Command Center for Combating Weapons of Mass Destruction to develop performance indicators and evaluation criteria.

[27]State's indicator is part of the annual Bureau Strategic and Resource Plan for the Bureau of International Security and Nonproliferation.

[28]CBP officials said they believe their Implementation Plan contained indicators. In our 2008 report, however, we found that although the plan contained expected goals and targets, they were not performance indicators.

officials said they conducted a formal evaluation of the two workshops they sponsored in 2009.[29] The report from the September 2009 workshop in Australia included some reporting of feedback from a written survey conducted at the end of the activity. Similarly, a CBP official provided examples of post-activity reports that include recommendations for future PSI efforts. However, these reports do not represent a systematic evaluation that links the activity results to the PSI objective. The officials with whom we met said they consider past activities when planning for the future, but they have no systematic evaluation of the activity results or impact to aid their planning. Further, the annual PSI reports to Congress do not generally document results of U.S. agencies' activities beyond the names of the participating countries.

Agency Officials Cited Challenges to Developing PSI Performance Measures

State and DOD officials cited a number of challenges to developing indicators to measure the impact or results of the U.S. government's PSI activities. According to the officials, results that can be quantified can also be misleading. For example, the officials stated the following:

- Tracking the overall number of new countries endorsing PSI ignores the fact that U.S. agencies have strategic reasons for focusing efforts on a certain country or subset of countries, even if a larger number of other countries might be persuaded more quickly to endorse.

- Tracking the number of interdictions does not necessarily link PSI activities to the initiative's objective. According to the officials, the initiative's activities are focused on building capacity to perform interdiction, but actual interdictions are not performed as part of PSI.[30] They emphasized that they cannot credit successful interdictions to PSI activities, in part because there are many efforts in addition to PSI that are focused on counterproliferation. Also, a change in the number of interdictions over the previous year could be attributed to a range of positive and negative factors, including better capacity to interdict, increased transfers of illicit material, or failure to deter transfers.

---

[29]FBI officials could not locate documentation of the evaluation report from the FBI-sponsored July 2009 workshop in Budapest, Hungary.

[30]Officials stated that although PSI complements and supports interdiction efforts, the act of performing interdictions is beyond the scope of PSI.

- Tracking measures of U.S. efforts, such as the number of activities hosted by the United States, ignores the fact that PSI is a multinational effort.

Further, State officials said some of the results of PSI activities are difficult to quantify. For example, although the officials said tools and expertise provided to participants at activities are used by participants to enhance their ability to interdict illicit cargo, the extent of the improvement is often difficult to measure and track.

Performance Measurement Possible Despite Challenges

Despite the challenges U.S. agencies face in developing performance indicators, it is possible for agencies to measure performance. One possible approach agencies could consider is to develop a framework that links PSI activities to the initiative's objective. GAO has previously identified such frameworks, called logic models, that agencies could adopt even if they face performance measurement challenges similar to some of the ones identified by PSI implementing agencies.[31] Specifically, GAO reported that using a logic model could allow the agencies to consider indirect outcomes and unquantifiable benefits when linking activities and outputs to the overall objective. By specifying the program's theory of what is expected, a logic model can help evaluators define measures of the program's progress toward its ultimate goals. In particular, GAO found that logic models were used or could be used to measure results in programs with challenges similar to some of PSI's, including, for example, difficulty in observing changes in behavior occurring after activity completion and difficulty in attributing outcomes to activities because of external factors' influence on the outcomes. Figure 1 provides generic guidance on how a logic model framework could be used to link agencies' program inputs and outputs to outcomes or impact. A logic model can help identify pertinent variables and how, when, and in whom they should be measured, as well as other factors that might affect program results.

---

[31]A logic model is an evaluation tool used to describe a program's—or initiative's, in the case of PSI—components and desired results and explain the strategy—or logic—by which the program is expected to achieve its goals. See GAO, *Program Evaluation: Strategies for Assessing How Information Dissemination Contributes to Agency Goals,* GAO-02-923 (Washington, D.C.: Sept. 30, 2002). For another example of how a logic model could be applied to a specific program or set of activities, see appendix IV in GAO, *Security Assistance: State and DOD Need to Assess How the Foreign Military Financing Program for Egypt Achieves U.S. Foreign Policy and Security Goals,* GAO-06-437 (Washington, D.C.: Apr. 11, 2006).

Figure 1: Sample Logic Model

Situation	Inputs	Outputs		Outcomes-Impact		
		Activities	**Participants**	**Short term**	**Medium**	**Long term**
	What we invest	What we do	Who we reach	What the short-term results are	What the medium-term results are	What the ultimate impact(s) is
	Staff	Workshops	Participants	**Learning**	**Action**	**Conditions**
	Volunteers	Meetings	Customers	Awareness	Behavior	Social
	Time	Counseling	Citizens	Knowledge	Practice	Economic
	Money	Facilitation		Attitudes	Decisions	Civil
	Materials	Assessments		Skills	Policies	Environmental
	Equipment	Product development		Opinions	Social action	
	Technology	Media work		Aspirations		
	Partners	Recruitment		Motivations		
		Training				

Environment
Influential factors

Source: Adapted from Taylor-Powell, E., Jones, L., & Henert, E. (2003) *Enhancing Program Performance with Logic Models.* Retrieved March 26, 2012, from the University of Wisconsin-Extension website: http://www.uwex.edu/ces/lmcourse.

A logic model can be used by agencies to guide their efforts to link activities to high-level objectives or impact, and agency officials could adapt the general framework to the individual program they plan to evaluate. For PSI, a logic model could link inputs and activities to outcomes while also documenting the challenges in measuring results. For example, officials could track quantitative inputs, such as the amount of money spent on a training activity about overcoming gaps in legal authority to interdict illicit shipments. They could link that input to measurable outputs, such as the number of participants trained. To link the outputs to short term results, they could make efforts to elicit feedback from participants to measure changes in participants' knowledge of ways to strengthen legal authorities. Agencies may be able to identify medium and long-term results, such as participants who successfully implement new national policies that strengthen their authority to perform interdictions. Together with the linkage of quantifiable measures, agencies could include narrative explanation of unquantifiable results that they believe contribute to the initiative's objective. They could also describe external factors that make it difficult to demonstrate or quantify the extent of the causal link between activities and results, such as the existence of other programs or initiatives that may also result in improved legal capacity to perform interdictions. Over time, the use of such a framework can help determine whether the results of the initiative's activities match the expected outcomes.

Federal agencies are increasingly expected to focus on achieving results and to demonstrate, in annual performance reports, how their activities help achieve agency or governmentwide goals. Because U.S. agencies have not developed indicators that can be used to measure systematically the results of their PSI activities, it is difficult for Congress and the public to know whether PSI activities hosted or participated in by the agencies are achieving their stated objective. As GAO has previously reported, in programs that inform and persuade others to act to achieve a desired outcome, it would seem all the more important to assure decision makers that this strategy is credible and likely to succeed.[32]

Conclusions

PSI has the potential to increase global capacity to recognize and interdict the flow of WMD, their delivery systems, and related materials on the ground, air, or sea, to and from states and nonstate actors of proliferation concern. The previous and current administrations have committed to implementing PSI and President Obama has called for it to be turned into a durable international institution. Given this commitment, it is important that agencies ensure that PSI is fully implemented according to legislative recommendations and requirements. Since our 2008 report, U.S. agencies have developed interagency PSI policies and procedures that satisfy a recommendation of the 9/11 Act. They have also submitted annual reports covering fiscal years 2008 through 2010 documenting their PSI activities, but these reports have not included the associated funding information for all PSI implementing agencies, as required by law. While all agencies we spoke with except DOD stated that they fund their PSI activities from their general funds, rather than request an annual PSI budget, it does not eliminate the requirement that they provide expenditure information for their PSI activities under the 9/11 Act. Without reports that include the required information for all agencies' PSI activities, Congress will not know how much the U.S. government is

---

[32]GAO-02-923.

spending on PSI and how such funds are being allocated. Also, while U.S. agencies have provided years of documentation of a range of activities they have performed or plan to perform under PSI, they have been unable to demonstrate if or how these activities are linked to the PSI objective. Without performance indicators that can be used to systematically measure progress toward the stated PSI objective and a framework for measuring the results of PSI activities, Congress and the public do not have a sufficient basis to judge whether PSI activities are successful.

Recommendations for Executive Action

To ensure that Congress has information to assess U.S. participation in PSI, we recommend that the Secretaries of Defense and State take the following two actions:

1. Include in the annual PSI report to Congress the required expenditure information for all U.S. agencies participating in PSI activities; and

2. Develop a framework for measuring PSI activities' results, including performance measures where possible that help link the results to PSI's objective.

Agency Comments and Our Evaluation

We provided a draft of this report to DOD, State, FBI, and DHS. DOD and State provided written comments on a draft of this report, which are reprinted in appendixes IV and V along with our responses to specific points. FBI and DHS, along with DOD and State provided technical comments that we have incorporated into this report, as appropriate.

In commenting on the draft report, DOD partially concurred with both of our recommendations. Consistent with our recommendation, DOD agreed that the annual PSI report should include expenditure information for all U.S. agencies. DOD stated that the reports have included information on expenditures by DOD and other agencies that are unique to PSI, while excluding items that are accounted for in agency general operating budgets. However, we found that some expenditure amounts not reported in the annual reports were unique to PSI and, therefore, should have been included. In a 2009 e-mail to CBP, a DOD official stated that travel expenses could be included in its submission to the annual report, as long as they were specifically for a PSI event. However, after CBP submitted such expenditures to DOD, they were excluded from the 2010 annual report even though they were for PSI-specific travel. DOD also partially concurred with our recommendation to develop a results framework. The department cited challenges in establishing objective and quantifiable measures of success but committed to make an effort to implement the recommendation by using the Critical Capabilities and Practices (CCP) concept as a results framework and to identify meaningful performance measures, where appropriate.

State partially concurred with the recommendation to provide expenditure information for all U.S. agencies participating in PSI activities. The department explained that it is difficult to define some expenditures as unique to PSI, for example, because travel in support of PSI events often coincides with travel in support of other department operational activities. However, the department said it would closely examine travel-related and other expenses unique to PSI in order to include them in future reports to Congress. State did not concur with our recommendation that it should develop a results framework. State said it had some indicators, such as the numbers of PSI-endorsing countries, for use in measuring PSI progress, but cautioned that PSI does not lend itself to collective data that would provide reasonable approximation of results. Nonetheless, State cited the CCP effort as one tool it intends to use, in coordination with other participating U.S. agencies, "which could contribute to an effective future analysis of the outcomes of coordinated PSI activity," which is consistent with our recommendation. Although we made a written request for documentation of State's PSI performance indicators in July 2011, State did not provide documentation of its PSI indicator and targets until March 2012, after it provided its response to our draft report. We have revised our report findings to include this documentation and our assessment. Upon reviewing the documentation provided, we found that the metrics State identified were not consistently listed as annual metrics in the strategic plan to which they refer. For example, neither the number of endorsing states nor the conclusion of shipboarding agreements were listed as metrics for fiscal years 2010 or 2011. In addition, State set no numeric targets for its participation in PSI activities for fiscal years 2010 or 2011. Without an overall results framework including, where possible, consistent indicators and targets that can be tracked over time, State cannot systematically evaluate its PSI activities.

We are sending copies of this report to the appropriate congressional committees, the Secretary of Defense, the Secretary of State, the Secretary of Homeland Security, the Attorney General, and other interested parties. In addition, this report is available at no charge on the GAO website at http://www.gao.gov.

If you or your staff members have any questions about this report, please contact me at (202) 512-9601 or melitot@gao.gov. Contact points for our Offices of Congressional Relations and Public Affairs may be found on the last page of this report. Key contributors are listed in appendix VI.

Thomas Melito
Director, International Affairs and Trade

List of Committees

The Honorable Carl Levin
Chairman
The Honorable John McCain
Ranking Member
Committee on Armed Services
United States Senate

The Honorable John Kerry
Chairman
The Honorable Richard G. Lugar
Ranking Member
Committee on Foreign Relations
United States Senate

The Honorable Howard P. McKeon
Chairman
The Honorable Adam Smith
Ranking Member
Committee on Armed Services
House of Representatives

The Honorable Ileana Ros-Lehtinen
Chairman
The Honorable Howard L. Berman
Ranking Member
Committee on Foreign Affairs
House of Representatives

Appendix I: Scope and Methodology

To assess the progress agencies have made since 2008 in establishing recommended Proliferation Security Initiative (PSI) policies and procedures, and issuing required annual reports, we reviewed the findings and recommendations in GAO's 2006 and 2008 reports on PSI and the Implementing Recommendations of the 9/11 Commission Act of 2007 (the 9/11 Act).[1] We requested and reviewed documentation of policies and procedures developed since 2008. Because the National Security Staff is the custodian of the interagency policy documents, we discussed the contents of those documents with National Security Staff officials and reviewed the documents to confirm that they contained PSI policies and procedures. We also reviewed PSI annual reports submitted to Congress by the Departments of State (State) and Defense (DOD) and analyzed them for compliance with the requirements in the 9/11 Act. We reported expenditure data as they appeared in the annual reports to Congress and discussed the reliability of the data with agency officials. We determined the data were sufficiently reliable for the purposes of our report. Further, we interviewed relevant agency officials to better understand the extent to which they implemented the requirements and recommendations in the 9/11 Act and any compliance challenges they faced.

To assess the extent to which PSI activities have enhanced and expanded U.S. efforts to prevent the flow of weapons of mass destruction (WMD) materials, we reviewed and analyzed documents from DOD, State, the Department of Homeland Security (DHS), and the Department of Justice (DOJ). We analyzed the information on each PSI activity in the annual reports covering fiscal years 2009 and 2010. We reported the number of PSI activities with U.S. participation based on agency documents. Because the agencies have not yet submitted the annual report for PSI activities in fiscal year 2011, we analyzed information on fiscal year 2011 activities provided by agency officials. We also interviewed relevant agency officials and solicited responses from seven DOD combatant commands to a list of questions about the PSI. In particular, we requested and analyzed documentation of actions relevant agencies have taken, if any, to develop indicators of PSI's success. In addition, we compared our findings with those of the 2008 GAO PSI review and reviewed GAO reports assessing agencies' evaluation frameworks and performance measurement.

---

[1]Pub. L. 110-53, sec. 1821.

For both objectives, we focused on DOD and State because the applicable recommendations and requirements in the mandate were addressed to them. In addition, we assessed DHS and DOJ progress because GAO made recommendations tc those agencies in 2008 to develop policies, procedures, and performance indicators because of the increased involvement of law enforcemert agencies in U.S. PSI efforts.

Appendix II: Full Text of the *Statement of Interdiction Principles*

The PSI is a response to the growing challenges posed by the proliferation of WMD, their delivery systems, and related materials worldwide. The PSI builds on efforts by the international community to prevent proliferation of such items, including existing treaties and regimes. It is consistent with, and a step in the implementation of the UN Security Council Presidential Statement of January 1992, which states that the proliferation of all WMD constitutes a threat to international peace and security, and underlines the need for member states of the UN to prevent proliferation. The PSI is also consistent with recent statements of the G8 and the European Union, establishing that more coherent and concerted efforts are needed to prevent the proliferation of WMD, their delivery systems, and related materials. PSI participants are deeply concerned about this threat and of the danger that these items could fall into the hands of terrorists and are committed to working together to stop the flow of these items to and from states and nonstate actors of proliferation concern.

The PSI seeks to involve, in some capacity, all states that have a stake in nonproliferation and the ability and willingness to take steps to stop the flow of such items at sea, in the air, or on land. The PSI also seeks cooperation from any state whose vessels, flags, ports, territorial waters, airspace, or land might be used for proliferation purposes by states and nonstate actors of proliferation concern. The increasingly aggressive efforts by proliferators to stand outside or to circumvent existing nonproliferation norms, and to profit from such trade, requires new and stronger actions by the international community. We look forward to working with all concerned states on measures they are able and willing to take in support of the PSI, as outlined in the following set of "Interdiction Principles."

Interdiction Principles for the Proliferation Security Initiative

PSI participants are committed to the following interdiction principles to establish a more coordinated and effective basis through which to impede and stop shipments of WMD, delivery systems, and related materials flowing to and from states and nonstate actors of proliferation concern, consistent with national legal authorities and relevant international law and frameworks, including the UN Security Council. They call on all states concerned with this threat to international peace and security to join in similarly committing to:

1. Undertake effective measures, either alone or in concert with other states, for interdicting the transfer or transport of WMD, their delivery systems, and related materials to and from states and nonstate actors

of proliferation concern. "States or nonstate actors of proliferation concern" generally refers to those countries or entities that the PSI participants involved establish should be subject to interdiction activities because they are engaged in proliferation through: (1) efforts to develop or acquire chemical, biological, or nuclear weapons and associated delivery systems; or (2) transfers (either selling, receiving, or facilitating) of WMD, their delivery systems, or related materials.

2. Adopt streamlined procedures for rapid exchange of relevant information concerning suspected proliferation activity, protecting the confidential character of classified information provided by other states as part of this initiative, dedicate appropriate resources and efforts to interdiction operations and capabilities, and maximize coordination among participants in interdiction efforts.

3. Review and work to strengthen their relevant national legal authorities where necessary to accomplish these objectives, and work to strengthen when necessary relevant international law and frameworks in appropriate ways to support these commitments.

4. Take specific actions in support of interdiction efforts regarding cargoes of WMD, their delivery systems, or related materials, to the extent their national legal authorities permit and consistent with their obligations under international law and frameworks, to include:

   a. Not to transport or assist in the transport of any such cargoes to or from states or nonstate actors of proliferation concern and not to allow any persons subject to their jurisdiction to do so.

   b. At their own initiative, or at the request and good cause shown by another state, to take action to board and search any vessel flying their flag in their internal waters or territorial seas, or areas beyond the territorial seas of any other state, that is reasonably suspected of transporting such cargoes to or from states or nonstate actors of proliferation concern, and to seize such cargoes that are identified.

   c. To seriously consider providing consent under the appropriate circumstances to the boarding and searching of its own flag vessels by other states, and to the seizure of such WMD-related cargoes in such vessels that may be identified by such states.

   d. To take appropriate actions to (1) stop and/or search in their internal waters, territorial seas, or contiguous zones (when declared) vessels that are reasonably suspected of carrying such cargoes to or from states or nonstate actors of proliferation concern and to seize such cargoes that are identified and (2) to enforce conditions on vessels entering or leaving their ports, internal waters, or territorial seas that are reasonably suspected of carrying such cargoes, such as requiring that such vessels be subject to boarding, search, and seizure of such cargoes prior to entry.

e. At their own initiative or upon the request and good cause shown by another state, to (a) require aircraft that are reasonably suspected of carrying such cargoes to or from states or nonstate actors of proliferation concern and that are transiting their airspace to land for inspection and seize any such cargoes that are identified and/or (b) deny aircraft reasonably suspected of carrying such cargoes transit rights through their airspace in advance of such flights.

f. If their ports, airfields, or other facilities are used as transshipment points for shipment of such cargoes to or from states or nonstate actors of proliferation concern, to inspect vessels, aircraft, or other modes of transport reasonably suspected of carrying such cargoes, and to seize such cargoes that are identified.

Appendix III: Proliferation Security Initiative Activities from Fiscal Year 2009 to December 2011

Month	Year	Type of activity	Event	Description	Location
Fiscal year 2012					
November	2011	meeting	OEG	Operational Experts Group (OEG) meeting	Germany
November	2011	exercise	Vigilant Shield	PSI portion of tabletop exercise	Norfolk, VA
Fiscal year 2011					
September	2011	other	Bilateral activity	Bilateral activity with Colombia	Colombia
August	2011	exercise	Panamax	PSI portion of live maritime exercise and tabletop exercise	Panama
June	2011	meeting and other	Regional OEG	Regional OEG meeting and Critical Capabilit es and Practices workshop	Honolulu, HI
May	2011	exercise	Phoenix Express	PSI portion of live maritime exercise	Mediterranean Sea
April	2011	exercise	Austere Challenge	PSI portion of live maritime exercise	Germany
April	2011	exercise	Saharan Express	PSI portion of live maritime exercise	Cape Verde/Senegal
April	2011	exercise and other	Bilateral activity	PSI tabletop exercise and workshop with St. Vincent and the Grenadines	St. Vincent and the Grenadines
February	2011	exercise and other	Bilateral activity	PSI tabletop exercise and workshop with Mongolia	Mongolia
November	2010	meeting	OEG	OEG meeting	Japan
October	2010	exercise and other	Eastern Endeavor	PSI portion of live maritime exercise and tabletop exercise; PSI workshop	Republic of Korea
Fiscal year 2010					
September	2010	meeting and exercise	Regional OEG / Pacific Protector	Regional OEG meeting and PSI portion of port exercise	Australia
May/June	2010	exercise	Phoenix Express	PSI portion of live maritime exercise	Mediterranean Sea
January	2010	exercise	Leading Edge	PSI portion of live maritime exercise, port exercise, and tabletop exercise	United Arab Emirates
October	2009	exercise	Deep Sabre	PSI portion of live maritime exercise, port exercise, and tabletop exercise	Singapore

Month	Year	Type of activity	Event	Description	Location
Fiscal year 2009					
September	2009	exercise	Panamax	PSI portion of live maritime exercise and tabletop exercise	Panama
September	2009	meeting and other	Regional OEG and counterproliferation workshop	Regional OEG meeting and 3-day workshop organized by FBI and Australia for PSI endorsing countries in Asia Pacific region	Australia
July	2009	other	Bilateral workshop	2-day workshop with Republic of Korea	Republic of Korea
July	2009	meeting and other	Regional OEG and counterproliferation workshop	Regional OEG meeting and 3-day workshop organized by FBI and Hungary for PSI endorsing countries in the Middle East and North Africa region	Hungary
June	2009	meeting	Regional OEG	Regional OEG meeting	Poland
May	2009	meeting	OEG	OEG meeting	Miami, FL
April	2009	exercise	Bilateral exercise	Bilateral tabletop exercise with Israel	Israel
April/May	2009	exercise	Phoenix Express	PSI portion of live maritime exercise	Mediterranean Sea

Source- GAO analysis based on DOD and State data.

Appendix IV: Comments from the Department of State

Note: GAO comments supplementing those in the report text appear at the end of this appendix.

United States Department of State

Chief Financial Officer

Washington, D.C. 20520

Mr. Loren Yager
Managing Director
International Affairs and Trade
Government Accountability Office
441 G Street, N.W.
Washington, D.C. 20548-0001

MAR 0 9 2012

Dear Mr. Yager:

We appreciate the opportunity to review your draft report, "PROLIFERATION SECURITY INITIATIVE: Agencies Have Adopted Policies and Procedures but Steps Needed to Meet Reporting Requirement and to Measure Results," GAO Job Code 120966.

The enclosed Department of State comments are provided for incorporation with this letter as an appendix to the final report.

If you have any questions concerning this response, please contact Kevin Pickard, Military Affairs Officer, Bureau of International Security and Nonproliferation at (202) 647-6320.

Sincerely,

James L. Millette

cc: GAO – Thomas Melito
ISN– Thomas Countryman
State/OIG – Evelyn Klemstine

Department of State Comments on GAO Draft Report

PROLIFERATION SECURITY INITIATIVE: Agencies Have Adopted Policies and Procedures but Steps Needed to Meet Reporting Requirement and to Measure Results
GAO-12-441, Job Code 320847

Thank you for giving the Department of State the opportunity to comment on the draft report entitled, "*PROLIFERATION SECURITY INITIATIVE: Agencies Have Adopted Policies and Procedures but Steps Needed to Meet Reporting Requirement and to Measure Results*." The comments below respond to the recommendations made in the GAO's draft report.

GAO Recommendation: Develop a framework for measuring PSI activities' results, including performance measures where possible that help link results to PSI's objectives.

See comment 1.

Response: The Department of State does not agree with the recommendation. The Department of State does maintain limited metrics on the progress and strength of the PSI as an activity. As mentioned in previous GAO reports, the Department can point to increases in the number of countries endorsing the PSI; the number and complexity of PSI exercises conducted around the world; and the conclusion of PSI ship boarding agreements as basic indicators to measure the Initiative's progress. These numbers are reported in the annual Strategic Plan of the Bureau of International Security and Nonproliferation (ISN).

The Department of State places great emphasis in ensuring the broadest support possible for this initiative. That is why the numbers of endorsing states remain a key measure of the relevance and health of the PSI. The only requirement for a country to participate in the PSI is to publically endorse the PSI Statement of Interdiction Principles. Therefore, the initiative, as designed, is an informal and voluntary association of countries committed to these Principles.   Not every country within the PSI will have the same capacity or capabilities to conduct WMD-related interdiction. Therefore, it is imperative that the PSI not "grade" or categorize specific levels of performance within the PSI.

2

GAO Recommendation: Include in the annual PSI report to Congress the
required expenditure information for all U.S. agencies participating in PSI
activities.

See comment 2.

Response: The Department of State partially agrees with the
recommendation. In previous reports to Congress, the Department of State
did not specifically detail the costs associated with travel related to uniquely
PSI activities because funding for such expenses comes from annual FY
appropriated operating funds. In addition, travel in support of PSI events
often coincides with travel in support of other Department operational
activities and is therefore difficult to define as travel expenses unique to the
Department's support of the PSI. Separate from associated travel expenses,
the Department of State provided only limited funding (less than $10,000) to
support of PSI events in FY2011. However, the Department will look
closely at specifically enumerating travel related and other expenses in
support of uniquely PSI events in order to include them in future budget
reports to Congress.

The comments below respond to statements made in various places in the
GAO's draft report.

GAO Statement: Despite recommendations in the 9/11 Act and by GAO
that agencies develop PSI performance indicators, DOD, State, CBP, and
FBI have not developed such measures and have not systematically
evaluated PSI activity results.

See comment 3.

Response: Standard Department of State procedures are followed regarding
indicators to measure program results for State's work on the PSI. As
previously mentioned, there are certain unclassified PSI activities that can be
quantified, which State uses as indicators to measure the Initiative's progress
as required in the annual Strategic Plan of the Bureau of International
Security and Nonproliferation (ISN). Although the Department considers
certain indicators that may provide rough measures of performance for U.S.
government PSI activity, it remains important to realize that the PSI, as
conceived and executed, does not lend itself to compiling collective data that
would provide a reasonable approximation of "results" as described in the
report.

Nevertheless, the Department, in coordination with other Executive branch
agencies, intends to utilize the Critical Capabilities and Practices (CCP)

3

effort as one tool which could contribute to an effective future analysis of
the "outcomes" of coordinated PSI activity. As mentioned in the report, the
CCP will seek to provide all PSI endorsing nations with a standard
framework for identifying the critical capabilities required to effectively
contribute to WMD interdiction operations and make available best
practices, lessons learned, and other tools and programs which can assist all
PSI countries in increasing their capacity to implement the PSI Statement of
Interdiction Principles.

GAO Statement: According to State officials, State does not identify and
track its PSI-related expenditures because its computer system does not
currently have the capability to do so. However, officials said they could
calculate State's total PSI-related expenditures because they are almost
entirely for travel to OEG meetings or bi-lateral negotiations.

See comment 4.

Response: This statement is incorrect. The ability of the Department to
identify and track PSI-related expenses is not an issue. Officials were trying
to explain that State, heretofore, has not decided that such a breakout is
necessary.

GAO Statement: The general characterization of Operational Experts
Groups (OEG) meetings as "planning meetings."

See comment 5.

Response: It is a misstatement to characterize OEG meetings as "planning
meetings." The OEG is essentially the steering committee for the initiative,
and the twenty-one participants of the OEG are generally best positioned to
routinely contribute to and host PSI activities, to share best practices, and
provide lessons learned on activities which support their PSI commitments
to each other and the other 77 countries which have endorsed the PSI. Aside
from providing an essential coordination function, the OEG meetings
provide the only venue of its kind where nations discuss counterproliferation
interdiction in a multinational setting.

The following are GAO's comments on the Department of State's letter,
dated March 9, 2012.

GAO Comments

1. Our recommendation focuses on developing a framework that links
   PSI activities to the initiative's objective, and not just on indicators,
   which alone do not link the activities to the desired outcomes.
   Although we made a written request for documentation of State's PSI
   performance indicators in July 2011, State did not provide
   documentation of its PSI indicator and targets until March 2012, after
   it provided its response to our draft report. We have revised our report
   findings to include this documentation and our assessment. Upon
   reviewing the documentation provided, we found that the metrics
   State identified were not consistently listed in its bureau strategic plan
   as annual metrics. For example, neither the number of endorsing
   states nor the conclusion of shipboarding agreements were listed as
   metrics for fiscal years 2010 and 2011. In addition, State set no
   numeric targets for its participation in PSI activities for fiscal years
   2010 and 2011. Without an overall results framework including, where
   possible, consistent indicators and targets that can be tracked over
   time, State cannot systematically evaluate its PSI activities.

2. State's decision to consider including PSI-specific expenditures in
   future reports to Congress is consistent with our recommendation.

3. If the Critical Capabilities and Practices (CCP) concept is developed
   as a framework that links PSI activities to outcomes and the objective
   of PSI, it will be consistent with our recommendation. (See also
   comment 1.)

4. Based on State's response, we have revised the report to reflect
   State's justification for not breaking out PSI expenditures. However,
   State's decision not to track PSI expenditures is inconsistent with the
   requirement to report such information annually.

5. The description of OEG meetings as planning meetings is consistent
   with our 2008 report on PSI. State concurred with this decision. In
   addition, we believe that the activities currently listed by State are
   consistent with PSI planning. We have added a footnote in the
   background more fully explaining OEG meetings.

Appendix V: Comments from the Department of Defense

Note: GAO comments supplementing those in the report text appear at the end of this appendix.

OFFICE OF THE ASSISTANT SECRETARY OF DEFENSE
2900 DEFENSE PENTAGON
WASHINGTON, DC 20301-2900

GLOBAL STRATEGIC
AFFAIRS

MAR   9 2012

MEMORANDUM FOR DIRECTOR, INTERNATIONAL AFFAIRS AND TRADE

SUBJECT: GAO DRAFT REPORT (GAO-12-441)

This is the Department of Defense (DoD) response to the GAO Draft Report, GAO-12-441, "PROLIFERATION SECURITY INITIATIVE: Agencies Have Adopted Policies and Procedures but Steps Needed to Meet Reporting Requirement and to Measure Results," dated February 17, 2012 (GAO Code 320847). Thank you for the opportunity to review the draft report. DoD's specific comments to the recommendations identified in the report are attached to this letter.

Rebecca K.C. Hersman
Deputy Assistant Secretary of Defense for
Countering Weapons of Mass Destruction

Attachment:
As stated

**GAO DRAFT REPORT DATED FEBRUARY 17, 2012
GAO-12-441 (GAO CODE 320847)**

**"PROLIFERATION SECURITY INITIATIVE: AGENCIES HAVE ADOPTED
POLICIES AND PROCEDURES BUT STEPS NEEDED TO MEET REPORTING
REQUIREMENT AND TO MEASURE RESULTS"**

**DEPARTMENT OF DEFENSE COMMENTS
TO THE GAO RECOMMENDATIONS**

RECOMMENDATION 1: To ensure that Congress has information to assess U.S.
participation in Proliferation Security Initiative (PSI). The GAO recommends that the
Secretary of Defense include in the annual PSI report to Congress the required
expenditure information for all U.S. agencies participating in PSI activities. (See page
20/GAO Draft Report.)

See comment 1.

DoD RESPONSE: DoD partially concurs with this recommendation. DoD agrees that
the report should include expenditure information for all U.S. agencies, and in the
coordination process to develop the report each agency is given the opportunity to submit
this information. Representatives from other agencies have supported PSI activities and
brought considerable expertise to PSI events. However, DoD believes that the report
should capture only those costs uniquely attributable to PSI. To that end, the report has
included information on expenditures by DoD and other agencies that are unique to PSI,
but it does not include items that are accounted for in agency general operating budgets
(e.g., TDY expenses, personnel salaries).

RECOMMENDATION 2: To ensure that Congress has information to assess U.S.
participation in Proliferation Security Initiative (PSI), the GAO recommends that the
Secretary of Defense to develop a framework for measuring PSI activities' results,
including performance measures where possible that help link results to PSI's objective.
(See page 20/GAO Draft Report.)

See comment 2.

DoD RESPONSE: DoD partially concurs with this recommendation. Since PSI is not a
formal program, but rather a set of activities, objective and quantifiable measures of
success may not be appropriate. Despite this challenge, we will work with our
interagency partners to determine if we can identify meaningful performance measures.
The Critical Capabilities and Practices (CCP) concept will provide a framework for
planning, executing, and subjectively measuring PSI activities, and we will work with our
interagency partners to determine how to use this framework to assess PSI activities
where appropriate.

2

The following are GAO's comments on the Department of Defense's letter, dated March 9, 2012.

GAO's Comments

1. The 9/11 Act requires that DOD, in conjunction with State, report to Congress annually on the amount expended for the prior year's PSI activities. Because DOD is the only agency we spoke with that makes a specific budget request for PSI-related activities, its decision not to report expenditure amounts accounted for in agency general operating budgets limits Congress' knowledge of the amount the U.S. government is spending on PSI and how those funds are being allocated. In addition, we found that some expenditure amounts not included in the annual reports were unique to PSI and, therefore, should have been included. In a 2009 email to CBP, a DOD official stated that travel expenses could be included in its submission to the annual report, as long as they were specifically for a PSI event. However, after CBP submitted such expenditures to DOD, they were excluded from the 2010 annual report even though they were for PSI-specific travel.

2. DOD's willingness to work with interagency partners toward developing and using a framework to assess PSI activities and toward identifying meaningful performance measures is consistent with our recommendation. If the CCP is developed as a framework that links PSI activities to outcomes and the objective of PSI, it will be consistent with our recommendation.

Appendix VI: GAO Contact and Staff Acknowledgments

GAO Contact	Thomas Melito, (202) 512-9601, or melitot@gao.gov
Staff Acknowledgments	In addition to the contact named above, Godwin Agbara (Assistant Director), Jeffrey Baldwin-Bott, Lynn Cothern, and Mattias Fenton made key contributions to this report. Martin de Alteriis, Mark Dowling, and Mary Moutsos also provided technical assistance.

GAO's Mission	The Government Accountability Office, the audit, evaluation, and investigative arm of Congress, exists to support Congress in meeting its constitutional responsibilities and to help improve the performance and accountability of the federal government for the American people. GAO examines the use of public funds; evaluates federal programs and policies; and provides analyses, recommendations, and other assistance to help Congress make informed oversight, policy, and funding decisions. GAO's commitment to good government is reflected in its core values of accountability, integrity, and reliability.
Obtaining Copies of GAO Reports and Testimony	The fastest and easiest way to obtain copies of GAO documents at no cost is through GAO's website (www.gao.gov). Each weekday afternoon, GAO posts on its website newly released reports, testimony, and correspondence. To have GAO e-mail you a list of newly posted Products, go to www.gao.gov and select "E-mail Updates."
Order by Phone	The price of each GAO publication reflects GAO's actual cost of production and distribution and depends on the number of pages in the publication and whether the publication is printed in color or black and white. Pricing and ordering information is posted on GAO's website, http://www.gao.gov/ordering.htm. Place orders by calling (202) 512-6000, toll free (866) 801-7077, or TDD (202) 512-2537. Orders may be paid for using American Express, Discover Card, MasterCard, Visa, check, or money order. Call for additional information.
Connect with GAO	Connect with GAO on Facebook, Flickr, Twitter, and YouTube. Subscribe to our RSS Feeds or E-mail Updates. Listen to our Podcasts. Visit GAO on the web at www.gao.gov.
To Report Fraud, Waste, and Abuse in Federal Programs	Contact: Website: www.gao.gov/fraudnet/fraudnet.htm E-mail: fraudnet@gao.gov Automated answering system: (800) 424-5454 or (202) 512-7470
Congressional Relations	Katherine Siggerud, Managing Director, siggerudk@gao.gov, (202) 512-4400, U.S. Government Accountability Office, 441 G Street NW, Room 7125, Washington, DC 20548
Public Affairs	Chuck Young, Managing Director, youngc1@gao.gov, (202) 512-4800 U.S. Government Accountability Office, 441 G Street NW, Room 7149 Washington, DC 20548

Please Print on Recycled Paper.